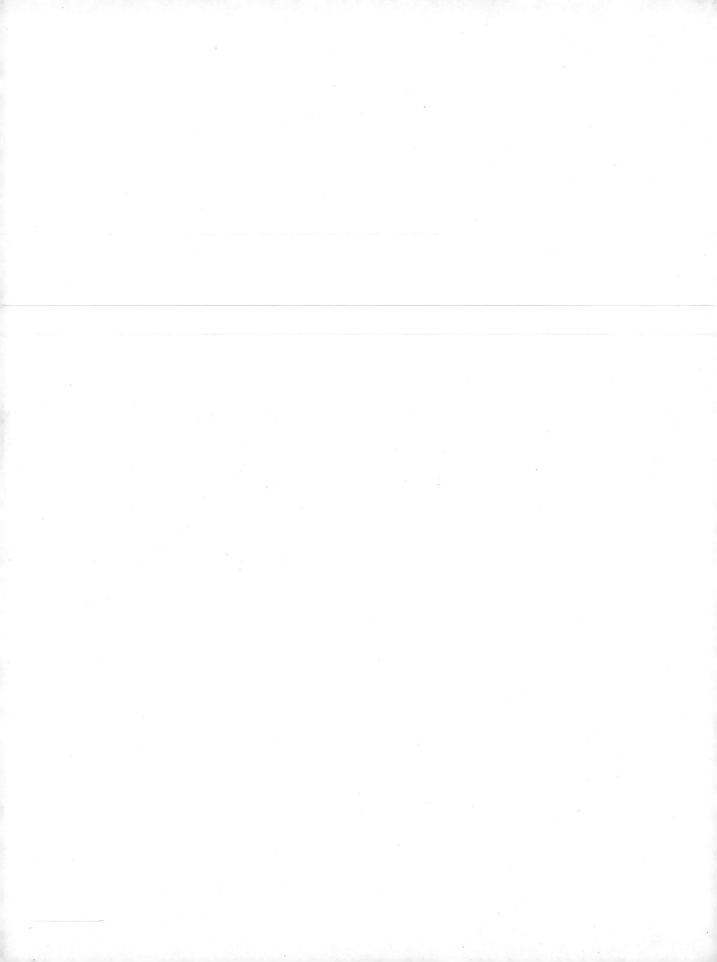

NATURE'S WRATH
THE SCIENCE BEHIND NATURAL DISASTERS

THE SCIENCE OF
VOLCANOES

ANGELA ROYSTON

Gareth Stevens
Publishing

Please visit our website, www.garethstevens.com. For a free color catalog of all our high-quality books, call toll free 1-800-542-2595 or fax 1-877-542-2596.

Library of Congress Cataloging-in-Publication Data

Royston, Angela, 1945-
The science of volcanoes / Angela Royston.
    pages cm. -- (Nature's wrath : the science behind natural disasters)
Includes bibliographical references and index.
ISBN 978-1-4339-8672-7 (paperback)
ISBN
ISBN 978-1-4339-8671-0 (library binding)
1. Volcanoes—Juvenile literature. 2. Volcanism—Juvenile literature. 3. Volcanologists—Juvenile literature. I. Title.
QE521.3.R685 2013
551.21—dc23

2012022953
First Edition

Published in 2013 by
Gareth Stevens Publishing
111 East 14th Street, Suite 349
New York, NY 10003

© 2013 Gareth Stevens Publishing

Produced by Calcium, www.calciumcreative.co.uk
Designed by Simon Borrough and Nick Leggett
Edited by Sarah Eason and Vicky Egan
Picture research by Susannah Jayes

Photo credits: Cover: Top: Shutterstock: Beboy; Bottom (l to r): Hawaii Volcano Observatory/USGS; Shutterstock: Mark Yarchoan, Pichugin Dmitry, J. Helgason, Vacclav. Inside: Dreamstime: Aask: 20c, Jiir Kulhanek 21b, Ollirg 13b, Radekdrewek 16tr, Lex Schmidt 41, Stormarn 44c, Swisshippo 35tr, Vulkanette 5b; Shutterstock: Gilles Baechler 8b, Brisbane 37bl, Moritz Buchty 29, John Copland 40tr, Sharon Day 43t, Pichugin Dmitry 17, Caleb Foster 45c, Gwoeii 1bc, 31tr, 36cl, 38b, Craig Hanson 4cr, J. Helgason 1tc, 30b, Laura Lohrman Moore 27t, Mopic 6tr, Ollirg 15cl, PavelSvoboda 32b, Roypix 33c, Robert Rozbora 42b, RZ_Design 13tr, Gian Salero 7, Thomas Sereda 10cl, Fredy Thuerig 28tr, Vacclav 39tl, Visdia 9t, Mark Yarchoan 11tr; US Geological Survey: 18c, 22-23, 23cl, 24cl, 24-25cl, 26br; Wikipedia: Hajotthu 14c, Lesto Kusumo.

Printed in the United States of America

CPSIA compliance information: Batch #CW13GS: For further information contact Gareth Stevens, New York, New York at 1-800-542-2595.

CONTENTS

WHAT IS A VOLCANO?

A volcano is a mountainous buildup of land that contains hot material from within Earth's crust. An erupting volcano is both spectacular and dangerous. Poisonous gases, hot ash, and molten rock spill out from a hole at the top of the volcano. The hot, liquid rock is called lava. As it flows down the side of the volcano, it cools to form solid, black rock. A volcano that is likely to erupt is described as "active." A volcano that is unlikely to erupt is described as "dormant," or sleeping.

Many volcanoes, including Mount Fuji in Japan, are shaped like a cone. Although Mount Fuji last erupted 300 years ago, scientists say it is still an active volcano. They warn that its next eruption could be very violent.

How Dangerous?

Some active volcanoes erupt gently most of the time. These eruptions do not threaten people in the surrounding area. Others volcanoes erupt only occasionally and are usually more violent and dangerous. A dormant volcano is one that has not erupted for hundreds or even thousands of years, but may erupt again. An extinct volcano is the safest type of volcano, because it will never erupt again.

When Mount Tambora in Indonesia erupted in 1815, it killed an estimated 92,000 people. During the eruption, the top of the mountain exploded, reducing the volcano's height by 4,000 feet (1,220 m).

Vent Inside the Volcano

In an active volcano, hot magma from inside the volcano rises up through a vent. This is a long channel inside the volcano that leads down into the earth. As the volcano becomes less active, a plug of solid lava blocks this vent. The bowl-shaped crater at the top of the volcano may then fill with water.

This photograph of Ertea Ale in Ethiopia, Africa, shows molten lava within the volcano's crater. Ertea Ale is an active volcano and it could erupt at any time.

CHAPTER ONE

VOLCANIC ERUPTIONS

Around the outside of the earth, under the oceans and continents, is a thin, solid crust of rock just 3 to 30 miles (5 to 50 km) thick. Below the crust, the rocks are so hot that they are molten. This hot, molten rock is called magma. A volcano forms at weak points in the earth's crust. Sometimes magma is forced up through this weak point, and it is then that the volcano erupts.

INSIDE A VOLCANO

Underneath a volcano, magma collects in a chamber in the rock. Sometimes a buildup of pressure under the ground pushes this magma up the main vent at the center of the volcano. As the pressure increases, side vents may open up off the main vent.

Finally, the magma erupts from the vents. Once out of the volcano, the molten rock is called lava. As the lava cools, it hardens into new rock around the cone, making the volcano even bigger and taller.

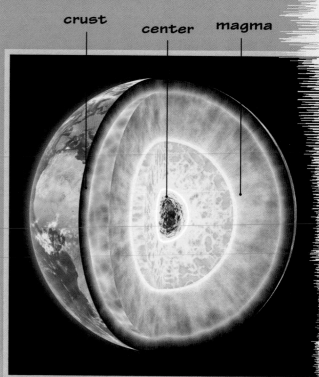

crust   center   magma

A cross-section of Earth shows what it is like inside. Beneath the thin crust is hot, liquid magma. At the center is hot, solid metal that is surrounded by molten metal.

WORLD'S WORST

Indonesia has more volcanoes than any other country. Of its 147 volcanoes, 79 are on the island of Java and 32 on the island of Sumatra. It has had 1,171 eruptions that scientists can date.

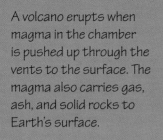

A volcano erupts when magma in the chamber is pushed up through the vents to the surface. The magma also carries gas, ash, and solid rocks to Earth's surface.

gas and volcanic ash

crater

lava

main vent

side vent

rock

magma chamber

WHAT CAUSES AN ERUPTION?

Movements in the earth's crust create volcanoes. The crust is made up of vast pieces of rock that fit together like the pieces of a jigsaw puzzle. The pieces, called tectonic plates, move very slowly all the time. Some plates crash together, others pull apart, and some slide alongside each other. Most volcanoes erupt where two tectonic plates either crash together or pull apart.

WORLD'S TALLEST

Mauna Kea on the island of Hawaii is the world's tallest volcano. It rises 13,796 feet (4,205 m) above sea level. Measured from its base on the seabed, however, Mauna Kea is more than 33,500 feet (10,200 m) high. This is taller than Mount Everest, the world's tallest mountain.

Mauna Loa

Mauna Kea

Mauna Kea has several craters around the summit. The volcano in the distance is Mauna Loa, which is only 115 feet (35 m) lower.

This model of Earth shows the edges of the tectonic plates as fiery lines. The line between South America and Africa is a ridge under the Atlantic Ocean. There the plates are moving apart.

ridge

What Moves the Plates?

The plates float on top of Earth's thick, liquid magma. As the magma slowly churns, it pushes the plates. The plates not only carry the land, but the seabed under the oceans, too.

Ring of Fire

Most of the world's active volcanoes are found around the edges of the Pacific Ocean, where they form what is called a "Ring of Fire." They curve from New Zealand up through the islands of Indonesia to Japan, and across to Alaska. They run back down the Pacific's east coast through the Cascade Mountains of North America and the Andes of South America.

9

TYPES OF ERUPTION

How violent a volcanic eruption is depends on the type of magma that it contains. An "explosive" volcano has thick, sticky magma with lots of gas trapped inside it. An "effusive" volcano is one that erupts steadily. It is filled with thick, runny magma, called lava, that contains a lesser amount of gas. It is the gas in the explosive volcano that creates an enormous explosion of volcanic material when the volcano erupts.

The small island of Stromboli in Italy is an explosive volcano. When it erupts, volcanic bombs and small pieces of hot magma explode in a fountain over the crater's top.

Exploding Gas

In an explosive volcano, the trapped gas heats up and explodes. The explosion blasts out chunks of solid material, called tephra. The largest chunks are as big as boulders and are known as volcanic bombs. The explosion can be so violent that these pieces of tephra are hurled many miles into the air.

When Krakatoa, in what is now Indonesia, erupted in 1883, it destroyed one-third of the island of Krakatoa. The sound of the explosion was heard 3,000 miles (4,800 km) away on an island near Mauritius—on the other side of the Indian Ocean.

Hot lava changes color as it cools. At its hottest, lava is yellow in color. As it cools, it turns dark red and then black. Even when lava turns black, it is still extremely hot.

Clouds of Ash and Dust

The smaller pieces of tephra that are released when a volcano erupts form thick clouds of ash and dust. These clouds of volcanic material can rise high into the air above the volcano and can be seen from many miles away before they fall back to the ground.

Lava Tube

Sometimes a natural tunnel, or tube, forms within the lava on a volcano's cone. The runny lava develops a crust that hardens. Under the crust a channel forms, through which runny lava rising up under pressure from inside the volcano continues to flow. Hot lava flows faster through a lava tube than on the surface of the mountain. This means that it travels farther down the mountainside before it breaks out of the end of the tube, and begins to slow down and cool.

REAL-LIFE SCIENCE
MOUNT ETNA, ITALY

Palermo

Mount
Etna

Mount Etna is a large volcano in eastern Sicily, Italy. It covers an area of 460 square miles (1,190 sq. km). Many people live in towns and villages on the slopes of the volcano.

Mount Etna, on the island of Sicily in southern Italy, is the highest and most active volcano in Europe. It has four craters and many side vents. Sometimes fountains of fire and clouds of ash explode from the volcano. At other times, huge flows of lava creep down the mountainside, threatening towns and villages. The nearby towns of Zafferana and Nicolosi, which are built on Etna's slopes, have been threatened by Etna's lava.

US Marine Major Jim Ross was on a helicopter that tried to stop lava from reaching Zafferana:

"It was a very challenging operation. We hovered just 15 feet (4.5 m) above the hot lava. I was swinging a concrete block below the helicopter, trying to push other concrete blocks into the hole in the lava tube. I don't think anyone believes you can stop the flow easily. It's not as easy as shoving a cork into a bottle."

Survivors Speak

Saving Zafferana

Zafferana is a small town on the eastern slope of Mount Etna. In December 1992, fountains of lava erupted and flowed downhill toward the town. Engineers built a huge wall 68 feet (21 m) high to hold back the lava, but the lava spilled over the top. Lava tubes formed, which allowed the lava to flow faster and much farther before cooling. Time was running out for Zafferana.

US helicopter crews tried to plug the lava tubes by dropping 7-ton (7-tonne) blocks of concrete into them, but the lava kept flowing and soon reached the edges of the town. Italian soldiers then dug a deep channel near the top of the main lava tube to divert the lava away from Zafferana. They used explosives to push the lava into the new channel. It worked, and the town was saved.

In December 1992, lava exploded violently from Mount Etna and threatened to overrun the town of Zafferana.

Mount Etna looms over the small town of Zafferana. The town has been rebuilt many times in the past, after being destroyed by the volcano's lava.

ETNA THREATENS NICOLOSI

In 2001, an effusive eruption began on July 17. It was followed a few days later by a series of violent explosions. Lumps of tephra shot hundreds of feet into the air. Flowing lava damaged the cable car station and continued toward the town of Nicolosi. Scientists said that the town was safe, but the mayor was angry that no help was offered. People began to panic and leave, but finally the flow stopped just outside the town. Nicolosi was safe at last.

Nothing in the path of a lava flow is safe. Homes caught in a flow can be almost completely submerged in lava.

500,000 Years Ago Etna First Erupts

MARCH 11–APRIL 15, 1669 Etna's most powerful eruption takes place. Multiple eruptions occur over the next few weeks. Lava covers 10 or more villages and reaches the city of Catania.

1852 A violent eruption covers 3 square miles (nearly 8 sq km) of the mountainside with hot lava.

NOV 4–6, 1928 The village of Mascali is destroyed by lava from Mount Etna.

1987 Two tourists are killed by an unexpected eruption near the summit.

DEC 14, 1991 Mount Etna erupts again, this time on the east side of the volcano. Lava flows for 473 days.

DEC 15, 1991 Lava flows downhill toward the town of Zafferana.

JAN 1992 A barrier 768 feet (234 m) in length and 68 feet (21 m) high is built to hold back the lava from the town.

Great Display

Today, Etna continues to erupt. It produces spectacular fiery fountains, lava flows, and explosions that can be seen and heard many miles away. On January 12–13, 2011, a fountain of lava 1,300 feet (400 m) high erupted into the night sky. However, Etna is not considered a dangerous volcano. Most eruptions do not spill far beyond the craters, and fewer than 80 people are known to have been killed in the last 2,700 years.

Ela Ziemba is an adventure hunter and photographer who spent two days and nights on Mount Etna:

"We spent a week in Nicolosi, a village about 7 miles (11 km) from the raging volcano. Volcanic ash was everywhere—in our food, hair, clothes, tent, and, worst of all, in our cameras. Then we decided to get much, much closer to the crater. We started to climb up the fierce mountain. After 10 hours we were unbelievably close! We heard the roar of the explosions. We saw huge rocks hurled very high and slamming back to the earth with a thud."

Mount Etna has many craters. This crater was formed when the volcano erupted in 1892.

FEB 1992 The lava breaks through the barrier. It flows rapidly down the mountain through lava tubes.

APRIL 1992 US Army helicopter crews drop concrete blocks onto the lava tubes to try to stop the flow.

MAY 23, 1992 Explosives divert the lava into a channel.

MARCH 1993 The flow of lava stops.

1993–2001 Etna continues to erupt at the summit.

JUL–AUG 2001 Lava damages the cable car station and threatens to overrun the town of Nicolosi.

2002–2003 Explosive eruptions create a thick column of ash. Earthquakes cause a landslide.

2003–2010 Eruptions continue.

2011–2012 Explosive eruptions produce ash clouds, lava fountains, and volcanic bombs.

CHAPTER TWO

VOLCANOLOGISTS AT WORK

For thousands of years, people did not understand why volcanoes erupted. Some believed it was because the gods were angry, some thought a volcano was the entrance to another world. However, people did recognize that when a volcano becomes more active, it is likely to erupt. The most obvious warning signs are earth tremors.

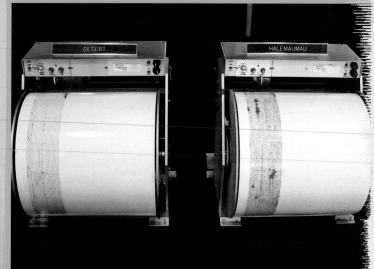

In a seismometer, the drum turns and shakes when the ground quakes. The pen remains steady and records the size of the tremors.

STUDYING VOLCANOES

Today, scientists called volcanologists study volcanoes in great detail, and try to accurately predict when volcanoes will erupt. They use many instruments to help them, including seismometers that detect and measure earth tremors. Instruments for detecting earth tremors have existed for centuries. As far back as AD 132, a Chinese philosopher named Chang Hêng invented the first seismoscope. This instrument showed the direction of an earth tremor, and could detect tremors up to 400 miles (644 km) away.

WORLD'S FIRST

Chang Hêng's seismoscope was a large container with eight dragon heads around the top. Each dragon head held a brass ball in its mouth, and directly below it was a toad. When the earth shook, the dragon head that was pointing toward the tremor dropped its ball into the toad's open mouth!

Volcanologists and tourists often visit White Island Volcano in New Zealand. Everyone wears a hard hat to protect them from falling ash and debris. The yellow substance in this photograph is sulfur, which spews from the volcano.

DANGEROUS WORK

Volcanologists want to know what is going on inside a volcano and when it is likely to erupt. The best way for them to find out is to get as close as possible to the action. This means climbing up the mountainside of a volcano and even entering the crater. Volcanoes can be unpredictable, and eruptions can occur with little warning. A volcanologist's job can be very dangerous.

This volcanologist is wearing a breathing mask and heavy boots. The mask allows her to get close to the crater so that she can measure the poisonous gases emitted there.

Hot Gear

Volcanologists wear specially adapted clothes that can withstand the hottest temperatures. In particular, they wear boots with thick soles to protect their feet from the hot ground. Even so, the heat makes their feet sweat! They may also wear hard hats, thick gloves, and protective suits, in case the volcano throws out large lumps of tephra.

Taking Samples

Volcanologists take samples from within the volcano's crater. They gather vital samples of lava and volcanic gases from the volcano they are studying and take them back to their laboratories for analysis. The information they obtain gives them clues about a volcano's behavior and can even tell them when and how the volcano may next erupt.

Safer Ground

Volcanologists work quickly on the volcano site and spend as little time as possible in the danger zone. Flying over a crater in a helicopter is a much safer way to gather data than climbing into the crater! Photographs of the crater and the volcano are taken. The photographs are then analyzed back at the volcano study center.

This volcanologist is collecting a sample of lava. The sample will help scientists to learn what is going on inside the volcano. As the lava bubbles out, it forms coils and other shapes that harden into rock.

In 2009, four volcanologists were lowered into the crater of Ertea Ale in Ethiopia, Africa. This active volcano is extremely dangerous. The volcanologists wanted to take a 3-D photograph of the crater. To set up the camera, they had to tiptoe over a thin crust of hot lava!

PREDICTING AN ERUPTION

There are more than 1,000 volcanoes around the world that are erupting now or are likely to erupt in the future. Scientists cannot monitor all of these volcanoes, since many may not erupt for 100 years or more. Instead, they monitor the volcanoes most likely to erupt soon.

This observation post in Kamchatka, Russia, contains a seismometer. The instrument records tremors to help scientists predict when the volcano may next erupt.

Early Warnings

Volcanologists look for three main signs that a volcano is about to erupt. The most obvious is an increase in earth tremors. Another is an increase in the amount of gases released by the volcano. An active volcano regularly releases gases from the crater and from side vents. Volcanologists monitor the amount of gases given off.

A particularly dangerous sign that a volcano is about to erupt is when the side of the volcano begins to bulge. This shows that magma is rising up from the magma chamber and that part of the mountainside is likely to explode very soon.

Type of Gases

Volcanologists not only measure the amount of gas escaping from a volcano, but also how much of each kind of gas is escaping. An increase in the amount of sulfur dioxide is often a sign that an eruption is rapidly building up inside the volcano.

Monitoring Lava

Scientists use many instruments to monitor different types of volcanoes. On an effusive volcano, such as Kilauea in Hawaii, an instrument is used to measure how much lava is moving through the lava tubes.

WORLD'S MOST UNEXPECTED

On February 20, 1943, a new volcano suddenly erupted in a cornfield near the village of Parícutin in Mexico. It terrified both the farmer who was working in the cornfield, and the villagers. By the next day, the volcano had formed a cone 164 feet (50 m) high! A year later it had grown to 1,100 feet (336 m), destroying the farm and Parícutin.

Gases are escaping from several vents on the side of this volcano. The yellow deposits show that some of these gases contain sulfur. If it is in the form of hydrogen sulfide, it will smell of rotten eggs!

REAL-LIFE SCIENCE
MOUNT SAINT HELENS, UNITED STATES, 1980

Mount Saint Helens is a volcano in the Cascade Mountains of Washington State, about 95 miles (153 km) south of Seattle. It had been quiet for 123 years. Then, in 1980, it erupted, devastating the surrounding area and killing 57 people. Scientists had been monitoring the volcano for several months before it erupted.

BEFORE

Seattle

Mount
Saint Helens

The ash cloud from
Mount Saint Helens
moved across the
United States
to the East Coast.

The Build-up

Earth tremors at the end of March 1980 alerted scientists that something was happening deep inside Mount Saint Helens. The tremors were followed by steam, which blasted through the ice in the crater at the summit. Volcanologists increased the number of seismometers in the area. Between March and May, the tremors increased and the mountain began to bulge near the summit. The volcanologists warned officials to evacuate the area.

The Eruption

On May 18, a major earthquake under the volcano caused the massive bulge to slip downhill. This was followed by a huge explosion that blasted rocks and ash into the air and outward over the countryside to the north. It triggered the biggest landslide in the area for many thousands of years.

The day before Mount Saint Helens erupted, its lower slopes were thickly covered with tall fir trees. The slope is bulging toward the camera.

AFTER

As mud poured down the mountain and along rivers, it snapped off and killed all trees in its path. Trees not in the path were undamaged.

Volcanologists Keith and Dorothy Stoffel were flying over Mount Saint Helens when it erupted. They only managed to avoid the huge ash cloud by quickly flying south:

"First we noticed rock and ice debris slide into the crater and, within a matter of seconds, the whole north side of the summit began to move. It rippled and churned, then began sliding to the north. We could take only a few pictures before a huge explosion blasted through the landslide."

TAKEN BY SURPRISE

Volcanologists knew that Mount Saint Helens was going to erupt explosively, but they did not predict just how big the explosion would be. The enormous eruption and the devastating fallout was far worse than anyone had ever anticipated.

No Chance

On May 18, the expert volcanologist David Johnston was camping at an observation post about 6 miles (10 km) north of the volcano. At 8:32 a.m. he radioed to the Volcano Center in Vancouver, "Vancouver! Vancouver! This is it!" Then the heat struck. His body was never found.

Four years after the eruption, Mount Saint Helens had a large crater created by the explosion. All the trees in the direction of the blast were destroyed.

4,500 Years Ago Mount Saint Helens First Erupts

1857–1980
Volcano is dormant.

MARCH 15–19, 1980 Several earth tremors are recorded.

MARCH 20, 1980 3:47 p.m. A strong earthquake occurs very close to Mount Saint Helens. Extra seismometers are set up to monitor activity.

MARCH 27, 1980 12:36 p.m. Following a loud explosion, gases and ash erupt from Mount Saint Helens.

MARCH 28– APRIL 18, 1980 Earthquakes and explosions of gas continue.

APRIL 29, 1980 The north side of the mountain begins to bulge near the summit. Safety zones are set up to keep the public away.

MAY 7–12, 1980 Earthquakes are felt. The bulge near the summit grows to 328 feet (100 m).

MAY 17, 1980 Property owners are allowed into the safety zones to collect their possessions.

MAY 18, 1980 8:32 a.m. An earthquake deep under Mount Saint Helens causes an eruption, which is quickly followed by a landslide.

Mudslide

Hot steam and lava melted the snow on the mountain. The water mixed with rocks, dust, and rubble from the landslide, creating a fast-flowing mudslide, which eventually reached the Cowlitz River 50 miles (80 km) away.

Ash Cloud

A thick cloud of ash blew eastward across the United States. It was so thick that in Spokane, 250 miles (400 km) east of the volcano, day became as dark as night. Ash and dust covered the ground, piling up very thickly near the volcano.

Angela Brown was a teenager living in Spokane when the volcano erupted:

"We could see the leading edge of the ash cloud. It was like a black window shade being pulled across the sky, wiping away the light of the sun. It quickly became as dark as night, yet it was still early afternoon. Ash began to fall as we neared home. Even in the short dash from the car to the house, the hot gusts of ash plastered our hair, skin, and clothes with gritty, gray particles."

Volcanologists can be seen here working in the large crater that appeared on the northern side of the volcano. The smoke behind them is coming from a new lava dome that is building up inside the crater.

Hot gases and bits of exploded mountain blast northward.

8:37 a.m. A hot blast reaches up to 23 miles (37 km) north of the volcano. A landslide of rocks, snow, and ice pours down the mountainside at up to 200 miles (320 km) per hour.

8:47 a.m. A cloud of ash reaches 15 miles (24 km) above the mountain and then blows eastward.

6:00 p.m. The ash cloud reaches the Great Plains 900 miles (1,500 km) away.

MAY 21, 1980 The ash cloud reaches the East Coast.

JUNE 2, 1980 The ash cloud is scattered around the Northern Hemisphere.

SEP 23–25, 2004 A new series of small earthquakes is recorded.

OCT 1, 2004– MARCH 8, 2005 Steam and ash erupt four times.

2005 ONWARD Small eruptions and tremors continue, and a new dome of lava builds up inside the crater of the volcano.

WARNING THE PUBLIC

People who live near volcanoes must rely on scientists to predict accurately when a volcanic eruption could threaten their lives. It is a difficult decision for volcanologists. If their alarms often turn out to be false, people will never believe them and thousands could be killed. Yet, officials should always take action if an alarm is issued—just in case disaster does occur.

Bad Advice

On November 13, 1985, Nevado del Ruiz in Colombia exploded, killing 23,000 people. An eruption in the afternoon had showered the town of Armero with ash, and the Red Cross told the townspeople to evacuate. Rather than heeding the warning and escaping from imminent disaster, the people stayed because the mayor and the local priest both said there was no danger. Just after 9:00 p.m. the volcano exploded again, even more violently. A hot mudslide descended on the town and buried Armero, killing nearly all of its residents.

Thick clouds of gas, dust, and ash erupt from Mount Pinatubo in 1991. This photo was taken from Clark Air Base, very close to the volcano. The gas cloud stretched as high as 22 miles (35 km) into the air.

Novarupta is one of several volcanoes in Katmai National Park in Alaska. Many are still active and are carefully monitored, but some, like this one, are extinct. The Novarupta crater has now filled with water.

WORLD'S WORST

The most powerful eruption was in 1912, when Novarupta erupted in southern Alaska. The eruption of Mount Pinatubo in 1991 was the second most powerful eruption in the twentieth century.

Thousands Saved

On June 15, 1991, Mount Pinatubo erupted in the Philippines. The explosion was 10 times more powerful than that of Mount Saint Helens. However, scientists had issued warnings, and the Philippine authorities acted quickly. They evacuated 60,000 people from the surrounding countryside, and 18,000 people were evacuated from a nearby United States' air base.

CHAPTER THREE

DANGEROUS FALLOUT

Explosive volcanoes can produce volcanic bombs, blasts of hot gases, and ash clouds—and that's just the start. The explosion can trigger mudslides and floods, too. Effusive eruptions, on the other hand, happen more slowly and are easier to deal with. The main danger from this type of volcano is hot lava flows.

Some lava flows, such as this one, are narrow, but others are wider. The speed at which lava travels varies, too.

UNSTOPPABLE LAVA

A mass of hot lava inching down a mountainside is an awesome sight. It moves slowly, but is unstoppable and destroys everything in its path, from buildings and automobiles to fields, farms, and even entire cities. Scientists work out the route that the lava is likely to take and where it may stop. If it is likely to overrun a town, it can sometimes be diverted.

WORLD'S WORST

When Mount Nyiragongo erupted in the Democratic Republic of Congo in 2002, lava flowed through the center of the city of Goma 11 miles (18 km) away. The flow split the city in half. Some 300,000 people were forced to flee, and 130,000 lost their homes.

Volcanic Gases

The gases that erupt from volcanoes are mostly steam mixed with several harmful gases. Sulfur dioxide, for example, has a strong smell and irritates the skin, eyes, nose, and throat. When it combines with sunlight and air, it produces a volcanic smog known as "vog."

The Sierra Negra volcano in the Galapagos Islands erupted in October 2005. The gases escaping from it contained so much sulfur dioxide that a volcanic smog spread for hundreds of miles over the Pacific Ocean.

HOT GAS AND ASH

When a volcano explodes, there is little that people who live nearby can do except flee. Exploding magma creates huge volcanic bombs, ash, and dust. However, by far the greatest killer is a pyroclastic flow. This is an enormous, toxic blast of extremely hot gas and dust that sweeps down the mountainside, destroying everything in its path.

Pyroclastic Flow

A pyroclastic flow can reach blisteringly hot temperatures of 400 to 1,300°F (200 to 700°C). These deadly flows burn everything in their path, including trees, automobiles, and buildings. Even if people and animals are not directly in the path of the pyroclastic flow, they may still be killed by breathing in the toxic, hot gas. The pyroclastic flow moves so fast that it is impossible to outrun it as it hurtles down the mountainside.

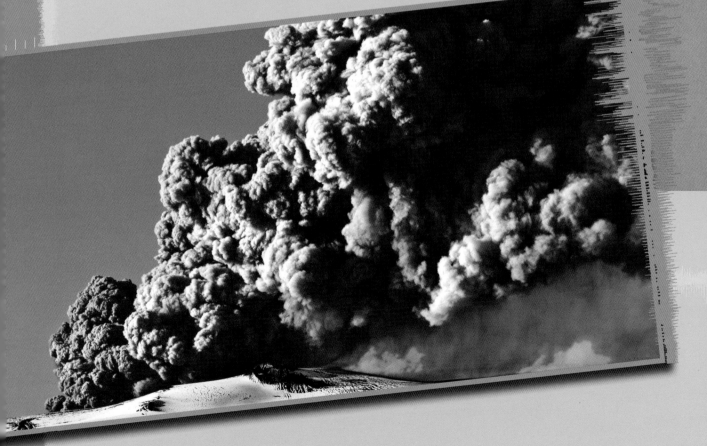

When Eyjafjallajökull erupted in April 2010, a vast ash cloud spread from Iceland across northern Europe. Aircraft were forbidden to fly, stranding hundreds of thousands of travelers far from home.

In April 2010, airline companies were keen to have the ban on flying in northern Europe lifted. Some pilots flew empty planes into the ash cloud to prove that it was now safe to do so. The ban was lifted on April 20.

Clouds of Ash

As a pyroclastic flow cools, it covers the ground with a thick layer of ash. Ash damages farmland, blocks waterways and roads, and clogs machinery. Ash clouds in the atmosphere endanger aircraft by clogging their engines. In April 2010, an ash cloud from a volcano in Iceland blew across northern Europe, grounding aircraft in 20 countries for six days.

WORLD'S WORST

Pyroclastic flows can travel up to 100 miles (160 km) per hour. In 1902, only two people out of 29,000 survived when a pyroclastic flow from Mount Pelée, on the Caribbean island of Martinique, swept through the port of Saint-Pierre.

31

MUDSLIDES AND FLOODS

When a volcano explodes, it may blow apart the top of the mountain and cause a landslide. This is when part of the mountain slides downhill. An enormous collapse of earth may turn into a deadly mudslide that destroys towns, cities, and farmland. Landslides can also trigger enormous tidal waves called tsunamis.

Mudslides

Many volcanoes are so high that they are covered in snow, even in places close to the equator. The heat of the eruption melts the snow, forming huge amounts of water. The water mixes with the landslide, producing a river of mud that flows fast downhill and covers everything in its path. The eruptions of both Mount Pinatubo and Nevado del Ruiz produced devastating mudslides.

The heat from this volcano in Iceland has melted much of the snow on the top of the mountain, creating the right conditions for a mudslide. Luckily, one big ingredient is missing from the mix—a landslide.

This car has been swept into a flooded river. Rivers quickly flood when large amounts of melted snow drain into them. If the river breaks its banks, the muddy water will flood onto surrounding land.

WORLD'S WORST

When Krakatoa erupted in 1883, so much of the mountain slid into the sea that it caused a tsunami up to 120 feet (37 m) high. The tsunami destroyed nearly 300 towns and villages on the islands of Java and Sumatra.

Floods

Water from melted snow can also pour down the mountainside, filling up rivers that then burst their banks. This results in enormous floods that can destroy crops, livestock, villages, and towns for miles around. As people become caught in the rush of floodwater, many will drown.

Tsunamis

Tsunamis are even more terrifying than floods. When a massive landslide plunges into a lake or the sea, it can set off a huge wave that sweeps across the water and does not stop when it reaches land. It flattens buildings and spreads debris along the countryside for many miles.

33

REAL-LIFE SCIENCE
MOUNT MERAPI, INDONESIA, 2010

Mount Merapi in central Java is the most active volcano in Indonesia. Hundreds of thousands of people live around the volcano and on its slopes. Merapi erupted in 1994 and again in 2006, but these eruptions were nothing compared to those in 2010.

Survivors Speak

Eno, who lives near Mount Merapi, tells what happened on October 26, 2010:

"I drove my grandmother, who lives about 6 to 9 miles (10 to 15 km) from the volcano, to a safer place. There were a lot of people trying to get out. I could feel the thick dust. It rained during the evacuation and when it stopped, ash and dust started to cover the ground. Some people stayed put in their homes as they were afraid their possessions would be taken."

This map of the Indonesian island of Java shows the location of Mount Merapi on its southern coast. When a volcano erupts, the damage is usually concentrated in one area.

Mount Merapi

The Volcano Becomes Restless

In late September and October 2010, volcanologists reported that Mount Merapi was becoming more active. Eruptions of gas and ash rose 2,600 feet (800 m) above the crater, and the number of earth tremors increased. On October 24, the government warned that a large eruption was likely. The next day, lava spilled down the mountainside.

Before it erupted in 2010, Mount Merapi was cone shaped. Clouds often formed above the tropical forest around its base.

Here, gas is seen escaping from the summit of the volcano. By late October 2010, gas and ash were exploding day after day, high into the air.

Powerful Eruptions

On October 26, columns of smoke rose 4,900 feet (1,500 m) above the crater, and pyroclastic flows raced down the mountain. Rescuers began to find the bodies of people killed by the eruptions. As the eruptions grew more powerful, many people fled from their homes. On October 30, flames shot up 6,500 feet (2,000 m) from the crater of the volcano and hot ash flowed down the mountainside.

35

THE DISASTER WORSENS

By November 2010, 42 people had been killed by the volcano and about 70,000 had lost their homes. Many people had injuries, such as burns, breathing problems, and eye irritations, but worse was to come.

Explosions and Mudslides

The eruptions became stronger. People were terrified by the loud explosions that scattered tephra, rocks, and dirt into the air. Hot ash flowed down the mountain. The pyroclastic flows reached more than 6 miles (10 km) from the crater. Then, on November 4, it started to rain heavily. The rain mixed with rocks, dust, and ash to create an enormous mudslide.

The homes of these Javan villagers were completely devastated by the huge eruption. Three months later, they were still waiting for their government to help them rebuild their houses.

Mount Merapi Erupts, 2010

OCT 24, 2010
The danger alert is raised to level 4.

OCT 25, 2010
The volcano erupts three times. Lava flows down the southern and southeastern slopes.

OCT 26, 2010
Pyroclastic flows start. The evacuation zone is 6 miles (10 km).

OCT 29, 2010
Lava and hot ash flow for 1.9 miles (3 km) down the mountainside.

OCT 30, 2010
The volcano erupts more powerfully. Ash shoots into the air and falls more than 19 miles (30 km) away. Mount Merapi then explodes.

NOV 1, 2010
Eruptions with loud explosions and hot clouds cause thousands of people to flee the area.

NOV 3, 2010
Pyroclastic flows travel up to 6 miles (10 km). Refugee camps are moved farther away. Ash clouds rise 16,000 feet (4,876 m).

NOV 4, 2010
Heavy rain mixes with exploded rocks, creating mudslides. An eruption occurs that is five times stronger than the one on October 26.

NOV 5, 2010
People within 12 miles (20 km) of the summit are told to evacuate. The death toll reaches 122.

Hadi Purnomo, District Chief of Sleman, a region near the volcano, reported:

"Many people, particularly young men, are trying to return to their homes to check on their livestock and property. We'll do everything we can to stop them, because the villages are death zones. There's no life there. The trees, farms, and houses are scorched. Everything is covered in heavy gray ash."

The pyroclastic flow left homes deep in mud and gray dust. This house is in Magelang province, 8.7 miles (14 km) from the volcano. Cleaning up after the eruption was a long and difficult task.

Backing Away

As the eruptions grew stronger, the government made the evacuation zone bigger. By November 5, people within 12 miles (20 km) of the summit were told to leave their homes. By November 9, 320,000 people were living in emergency shelters. Volcanologists, too, had moved farther from the mountain. On November 10, the eruptions began to die down, but for the survivors of the disaster the task of rebuilding their lives had only just begun.

NOV 6–9, 2010
Severe eruptions continue. The death toll reaches more than 153 people, including four rescuers.

NOV 10, 2010
The level of volcanic activity begins to fall, but eruptions of hot air, ash, and lava continue from time to time.

DEC 3, 2010
The danger alert is reduced to level 3. The danger zone is reduced to 1.6 miles (2.5 km). The number of people dead reaches 353.

RESCUE AND REBUILDING

Once a village has been covered with lava or mud from a volcanic explosion, it is usually too late to save many people who live there. The best way to save people is to evacuate the danger zone before the eruption overwhelms them. Even then, thousands of people may lose their homes, farms, and communities. The devastation can be so great that many people never return to the area where they lived.

Reaching the Injured

Getting to the worst-affected areas can take days. Highways may be blocked by lava, mud, or ash, and the heat makes it hard for rescuers to reach survivors. When homes are covered by mud, people dig in the hope of finding anyone alive. Sometimes, amazingly, the rescuers are successful.

When Mount Vesuvius in Italy erupted in AD 79, the cities of Pompeii and Herculaneum were covered in thick ash. Many people died. In 1749, the city was unearthed, along with the preserved imprints of its inhabitants.

Villagers were still clearing out ash from their shops and homes in Magelang province four months after Mount Merapi erupted. Some of the ash was piled up into steep banks so that vehicles had better access.

WORLD'S WORST

In 1997, a volcano on the Caribbean island of Montserrat erupted and covered Plymouth, the island's capital, with thick, hot ash. Plymouth is still in ruins, inside the evacuation zone around the volcano. People live crowded together at the other end of the island. Many have left the island forever.

Buried Alive

Survivors may be pulled out alive from within homes that have been submerged beneath a mudslide. Incredibly, sometimes survivors have managed to find a small pocket of air in which they could stay alive for a few hours until they are rescued.

Medical Help

Survivors may be injured, particularly if they were close to a pyroclastic flow. Volcanic gases, hot ash, and dust damage people's lungs, skin, and eyes. Doctors and nurses treat burns, breathing difficulties, eye irritations, and other injuries.

CHAPTER FOUR

NOT ALL BAD NEWS

Volcanoes can be deadly, so why do so many people live on their slopes and at their feet? The answer is that volcanoes bring benefits as well as dangers. The soil is very fertile, which means it is good for growing crops, and volcanic rocks often contain valuable minerals. Some volcanoes can supply electricity and free hot water. On a larger scale, volcanoes create mountains, islands, and much of our land.

On Lanzarote in the Canary Islands, farmers grow crops in the rich, volcanic soil.

FERTILE EARTH

Some of the most fertile soils in the world are formed on volcanoes. As lava and ash eventually break down, they form soil that contains minerals and other nutrients that help plants to grow. Volcanic ash that is blown far from a volcano also helps to improve and fertilize the soil it falls on.

Volcanic Rocks

Magma contains metals such as gold, silver, copper, and tin. The rocks on a volcano often contain concentrated amounts of these and other minerals. These precious metals are used to make sheets of metal, jewels, and other items.

WORLD'S MOST POPULAR

Tourists are fascinated by volcanoes. Hawaii Volcanoes National Park has not one, but two volcanoes—Kilauea, which erupts continually, and Mauna Loa, the world's highest volcano. These volcanoes attract about 3 million tourists every year.

There is always some exciting volcanic action to see on Mount Etna. Each year, many tourists climb to the summit to get an amazing view of the main crater.

HOT SPRINGS

When a volcano erupts, the heat that escapes from the crater is uncontrolled and dangerous. However, people have found ways to use the heat from some volcanoes in a controlled way. A geyser is a volcano from which boiling hot water erupts, instead of lava. The hot water can be piped to the homes and buildings of people who live nearby or may be used to make electricity in a geothermal power station.

Free Hot Water

Several countries have geysers. In Iceland, the hot water from the country's many geysers is piped into people's homes, where it is used for central heating and to heat swimming pools. New Zealand and the United States have hot geysers, too. In New Zealand, people used to cook food on the geysers. When Europeans arrived, they found free hot water for washing and heating. Sadly, they took too much and now most of the geysers have dried up.

In Iceland, the temperature of the water from geysers is even suitable for swimming in. People often relax in enormous pools surrounded by snow!

The world's biggest geothermal power station is in Mexicali, in Baja California, Mexico. The largest group of power stations is in northern California. Called the Geysers, it consists of 15 geothermal power stations.

Old Faithful in Yellowstone National Park is one of the most famous geysers in the world. It erupts around every 90 minutes.

Geothermal Power

The largest geothermal power stations use heat from steaming geysers to turn a turbine to generate electricity. The electricity is then sent via cables to power local homes, business offices, and even factories. Geothermal power stations can generate electricity day and night, all year, making them a reliable energy source.

Endless Steam

Geothermal power is sustainable if it is managed well. The hot water will continue forever—provided it is not taken out faster than it is renewed by the volcano's natural processes. Fuels such as coal, oil, and gas are not sustainable. The processes that produced these fuels took millions of years, so they cannot be renewed.

43

MAKING NEW LAND

Much of the land we live on is shaped and created by volcanoes. Some volcanoes rise up to tower over a surrounding plain, while many others form part of long mountain ranges, such as the Andes that run the length of South America. Many islands are actually the tops of volcanoes. As volcanoes on the seabed grow, they eventually rise above the surface of the sea, creating islands. The islands of Hawaii are the tops of underwater volcanoes.

Sincholagua in Ecuador is a mountain peak in the high Andes Mountains of South America. It is an extinct volcano and its summit has been worn away by the weather.

Making Mountains

The world's longest volcanic mountain ranges, however, are under the sea. They form ridges, such as the Mid-Atlantic Ridge on the floor of the Atlantic Ocean. Volcanic activity is making this ridge in particular grow bigger and, as it grows, it is slowly pushing North and South America farther away from Europe and Africa.

Hot Spot Islands

It usually takes many millions of years for undersea volcanoes to grow so tall that they appear above the surface of the sea, creating volcanic islands. The tallest volcanoes form over a "hot spot," a place from which magma has erupted for millions of years.

Volcanoes are part of Earth's ever-changing landscape. We cannot control volcanoes or prevent their eruptions, but by studying these violent forces of nature we can better forecast if, and when, they may erupt once more.

The islands of Hawaii in the Pacific Ocean are just one group of volcanic islands. The landscape varies from steep rock faces to valleys of tropical rain forest.

GLOSSARY

active volcano: a volcano that is erupting or could erupt

debris: sections of magma, rock, and soil broken up by a volcanic explosion

dormant volcano: a volcano that has not erupted for a long time but may erupt again

earth tremor: shaking of the ground caused by forces under Earth's crust

effusive volcano: a volcano that erupts steadily

erupt: explode

evacuation zone: an area around an erupting volcano, or other danger, from which people are told to leave

explosive volcano: a volcano that erupts suddenly and violently

extinct volcano: a volcano that is no longer active or dormant

fertile: good for growing crops or other plants

geothermal power: electricity made using heat from inside the earth

geyser: a fountain of hot water that erupts from under the ground

lava: magma that has reached Earth's surface

magma: hot, liquid rock inside a volcano or underneath Earth's crust

molten: melted by great heat

nutrient: substance, such as a mineral, that helps plants to grow

pyroclastic flow: a cloud of hot gas, ash, and rocks that flows very fast down the side of a volcano

seismometer: an instrument for measuring and recording the size of earth tremors and the time they occur

seismoscope: an instrument for detecting earth tremors and their directions

sustainable: able to continue without running out

tectonic plate: section of Earth's crust that carries the continents and seabed

tephra: solid material thrown out by an explosive volcano

tsunami: a huge wave created by an undersea volcano, an earthquake, or a landslide from a volcano

turbine: piece of machinery that turns, generating electricity

vent: an opening

volcanologist: scientist who studies volcanoes

FOR MORE INFORMATION

Books

Fradin, Judy and Dennis. *Volcano! The Icelandic Eruption of 2010 & Other Hot, Smoky, Fierce, and Fiery Mountains*. Washington, DC: National Geographic, 2010.

Landau, Elaine. *Volcanoes*. New York, NY: Children's Press, 2009.

Spilsbury, Louise and Richard. *Violent Volcanoes*. Chicago, IL: Heinemann Library, 2010.

Van Rose, Susanna. *Volcano & Earthquake*. New York, NY: DK Publishing, 2004.

Websites

Find out how volcanoes are formed and why and how they explode.
science.howstuffworks.com/nature/natural-disasters/volcano.htm

Discover more about volcanoes and their great dangers.
volcanoes.usgs.gov/hazards/index.php

Find out what it's like to live with a volcano in your backyard.
vulcan.wr.usgs.gov/Outreach/Publications/GIP19/framework.html

Learn more about the hazards of volcanoes.
pubs.usgs.gov/fs/fs002-97

Take a look at some amazing volcanoes photos.
vulcan.wr.usgs.gov/Photo/framework.html

Publisher's note to educators and parents: Our editors have carefully reviewed these websites to ensure that they are suitable for students. Many websites change frequently, however, and we cannot guarantee that a site's future contents will continue to meet our high standards of quality and educational value. Be advised that students should be closely supervised whenever they access the Internet.

48